DK EYEWITNESS WORKBOOKS

Ancient Rome

by Sue Nicholson

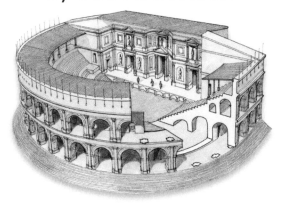

Educational Consultant Linda B. Gambrell,
Distinguished Professor of Education,
Clemson University

Senior Editors Jane Yorke, Fleur Star
Project Editor Sue Malyan
Senior Art Editor Owen Peyton-Jones
Editor Nayan Keshan
US Editor Megan Douglass
Art Editors Tanisha Mandal, Peter Radcliffe
Managing Editors Christine Stroyan, Shikha Kulkarni
Managing Art Editors Anna Hall, Govind Mittal
DTP Designer Anita Yadav
Production Editor Tom Morse
Production Controller Nancy-Jane Maun
Senior Jacket Designer Suhita Dharamjit
Jacket Design Development Manager Sophia MTT
Publisher Andrew Macintyre
Art Director Karen Self
Publishing Director Jonathan Metcalf

This American Edition, 2020
First American Edition, 2007
Published in the United States by DK Publishing
1450 Broadway, Suite 801, New York, NY 10018

Copyright © 2007, 2020 Dorling Kindersley Limited
DK, a Division of Penguin Random House LLC
20 21 22 23 24 10 9 8 7 6 5 4 3 2 1
001-323010-Jun/2020

A catalog record for this book
is available from the Library of Congress.
ISBN: 978-0-7440-3450-9

DK books are available at special discounts when purchased in bulk
for sales promotions, premiums, fund-raising, or educational use.
For details, contact: DK Publishing Special Markets,
1450 Broadway, Suite 801, New York, NY 10018
SpecialSales@dk.com

Printed and bound in Canada

For the curious

www.dk.com

Contents

Fast Facts

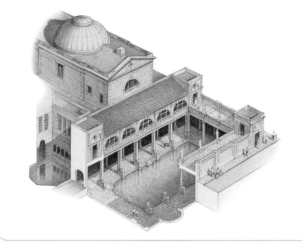

Activities

Quick Quiz

How This Book Can Help Your Child

The **Eyewitness Workbooks** series offers a fun and colorful range of stimulating titles on the subjects of history, science, and geography. Devised and written with the expert advice of educational consultants, each workbook aims to:

- develop a child's knowledge of a popular topic
- provide practice of key skills and reinforce classroom learning
- nurture a child's special interest in a subject

About this book

Eyewitness Workbook Ancient Rome is an activity-packed exploration of people and places in Ancient Rome. Inside you will find:

Fast Facts

This section presents key information as concise facts that are easy to digest, learn, and remember. Encourage your child to start by reading through the valuable information in the Fast Facts section and studying the statistics charts at the back of the book before trying out the activities.

Activities

The enjoyable, fill-in activities are designed to develop information recall and help your child practice cross-referencing skills. Each activity can be completed using information provided on the page, in the Fast Facts section, or on the charts at the back of the book.

Quick Quiz

There are six pages of multiple-choice questions to test your child's newfound knowledge of the subject. Children should only try answering the quiz questions once all of the activity section has been completed. As your child finishes each page of themed questions, check the answers together.

Important information

- The dates in this book are written as BCE ("Before the Common Era") and CE ("in the Common Era"). BCE is comparable to BC, or "Before Christ," so 500 BCE is the same as 500 BC. CE is comparable to AD, or "Anno Domini," which is Latin for "the year of the Lord," so 500 CE is the same as AD 500.

- Supervise your child when he or she is doing the cooking activity on page 31, and help with cutting out the fabric in the "Making a toga" activity on page 29. Also make sure that your child takes care using scissors in the "Make a mosaic" activity on page 27.

PROGRESS CHART

Chart your progress as you work through the activity and quiz pages in this book. First check your answers, then color in a star in the correct box below.

Page	Topic	Star	Page	Topic	Star	Page	Topic	Star
14	Key Dates in Ancient Rome	☆	24	Roman Homes	☆	34	Entertainment	☆
15	Key Dates in Ancient Rome	☆	25	Roman Homes	☆	35	Gladiator Fights	☆
16	The City of Rome	☆	26	Roman Art	☆	36	Gods and Goddesses	☆
17	Roman Ruins	☆	27	Mosaics	☆	37	Priests and Sacrifice	☆
18	Hail Caesar!	☆	28	Roman Fashion	☆	38	History of Ancient Rome	☆
19	Emperors of Rome	☆	29	Roman Fashion	☆	39	Rulers and Citizens	☆
20	Trade Across the Empire	☆	30	Food and Drink	☆	40	The Roman Army	☆
21	Money Matters	☆	31	A Roman Feast	☆	41	Travel and Cities	☆
22	A Legionnaire's Life	☆	32	Roman Writing	☆	42	Money and Trade	☆
23	Into Battle	☆	33	Roman Writing	☆	43	Daily Life	☆

Early Rome

The Roman Empire was one of the biggest and best-organized empires in history. It began more than two thousand years ago, with the founding of the city of Rome in the country now called Italy. The early Roman civilization was influenced by two neighboring peoples—the Etruscans and the Greeks.

Statue of the she-wolf suckling
Romulus and Remus

Founding Rome

According to legend, Rome was founded in 753 BCE by twin brothers, Romulus and Remus. It was built on seven hills beside the Tiber River, on the borders of the kingdom of Etruria.

Key facts

- Romulus and Remus were said to be sons of the war god, Mars.
- As babies, the twins had been left out to die but, according to the legend, they were found by a she-wolf, who took care of them.
- When they were grown up and were founding the city, the twins argued, and Romulus killed Remus.
- Romulus then gave his name to the city they had founded, and became the first ruler of Rome.

The Etruscans

The Etruscan people lived in a group of city-states in northern Italy. Rome came under Etruscan influence very early and several of its kings were Etruscans until the Roman nobles threw out the last of them, called Tarquin the Proud, in 509 BCE.

Key facts

- The Etruscans may have come from Asia Minor (now Turkey) before they settled in Italy.

Etruscan sculpted
cremation urn

- They were skilled at metal-working and traded in bronze, iron, and precious metals.
- The Etruscans were also great architects and engineers. They built Rome's first drainage system.
- The Roman toga was based on robes worn by the Etruscans.

The Greeks

The Romans were also influenced by the Greek civilization. The Greeks had founded cities across southern Italy. Many of the cities were wealthy, with elegant houses and beautiful temples.

The Romans built temples based on
ancient Greek designs.

Key facts

- The Romans admired and copied the realistic figures in Greek art and sculpture.
- Many Roman gods are based on Greek gods. For example, the Roman goddess of love, Venus, is similar to the Greek goddess of love, Aphrodite.
- The Roman poet Virgil modeled his most famous work, the *Aeneid*, on the epic poems the *Iliad* and the *Odyssey*, by the Greek writer Homer.
- Roman theaters are similar to Greek theaters. The seats are arranged in a huge semi-circle, looking down onto a stage.

Ruins of a Greek theater in
southern Italy

Roman Conquest

The Romans fought many wars and gradually ruled more and more land. They built towns and roads, and spread their way of life throughout the areas they ruled. By 284 BCE they had defeated the Etruscans, Gauls, and Samnites (tribes who lived in northern and central Italy). During the Pyrrhic Wars, the Romans fought and defeated King Pyrrhus of Greece to gain control of southern Italy. By 264 BCE, Rome ruled all of Italy.

The Punic Wars

The Roman Empire at its height, in 117 CE

In 264–146 BCE, Rome fought the people of Carthage in a series of wars called the Punic Wars. The Carthaginians controlled lands around the western part of the Mediterranean Sea. Their main city was Carthage, on the coast of North Africa.

Key facts

- In 218 BCE a Carthaginian general called Hannibal marched his army, and 37 elephants, over the mountains into Italy.
- Hannibal won many battles in Italy but he did not conquer the city of Rome. He was later defeated at a battle in Africa.
- The Punic Wars ended when the Romans defeated the people of Carthage in 146 BCE.

Coin showing the head of Hannibal

Height of the empire

After the wars with Carthage, the whole of the Mediterranean area was ruled by the Romans. The Romans then fought wars with tribes farther away. The empire was at its most powerful by the 2nd century CE.

Key facts

- At its height, the Roman Empire covered an area measuring 2,300 miles (3,700 km) from north to south, and 2,500 miles (4,000 km) from east to west.
- The Romans are the only people in history to have ruled all the lands around the Mediterranean Sea.
- The Romans divided their empire into different provinces.
- In 43 CE the Romans invaded southern Britain.

End of the empire

Because the Roman Empire was so vast, it was hard to rule. There were attacks from tribes including the Goths in the north, and from Persians in the east. There were also civil wars in Rome as various generals struggled for power.

Small statue of a 7th century Byzantine emperor

Key facts

- In 284 CE, the Empire was divided into two parts, east and west.
- Emperor Constantine I reunited the empire during his rule (324–337 CE), but it split up again when he died.
- Much of the western part of the Roman Empire was overrun by Germanic tribes in 406 CE. In that year, Roman troops left Britain to defend Rome.
- The city of Rome was invaded in 410 CE, and the last emperor in the west lost power in 476 CE.
- The eastern empire (called the Byzantine Empire) continued until 1453 CE.

Roman rulers

After the Romans expelled the last Etruscan king in 509 BCE, Rome became a republic. It was ruled by an appointed group for nearly 500 years. In 27 BCE, a man called Octavian became the most powerful senator. He took the name *Imperator Caesar Augustus*, and became the first emperor of Rome. Rome was then ruled by emperors for the next 500 years.

The senate

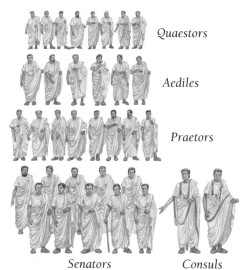

Quaestors

Aediles

Praetors

Senators   Consuls

Roman senators

Senators were appointed by the consuls and usually served on the senate for life. At first, there were 100 senators. Later, there were 600.

Key facts

- In the republic, two senators were elected each year to be consuls and rule in place of a king.
- *Quaestors* were in charge of finance; *Aediles* looked after the streets, public buildings, and markets; and *Praetors* dealt with justice.
- In an emergency, the senate could nominate a dictator to rule Rome alone for up to six months.

Julius Caesar

During the 1st century BCE, there was a series of civil wars in which ambitious senators fought each other for power. In 48 BCE, a brilliant general and consul called Julius Caesar defeated his rival Pompey (another consul), and made himself ruler of Rome.

Key facts

- Caesar ruled like a king, which made him unpopular.
- During his rule, he issued coins showing his portrait. This was an honor normally given to famous Romans only after their death.
- Caesar was stabbed to death on March 15, 44 BCE, by a group of senators who wanted to restore the republic. He died at the foot of a statue of Pompey.

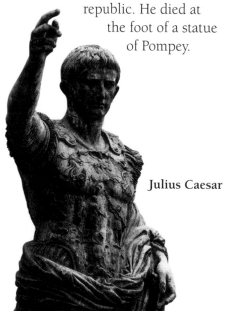

Julius Caesar

The first emperor

After Caesar's death, his friend Mark Antony and Caesar's adopted son Octavian divided the Roman Empire between them. But they soon became enemies and there was civil war. This ended when Octavian defeated Antony in battle. Octavian then became Augustus, the first emperor of Rome.

Augustus, the first emperor of Rome

Key facts

- Augustus ruled from 27 BCE to 14 CE. He was popular because he brought peace after many years of fighting.
- Augustus was a great leader and administrator. He also supported literature and the arts.
- His title was *Imperator Caesar Augustus. Imperator* means "commander" and is the origin of our word emperor. *Augustus* means "majestic" or "venerable."
- Augustus formed a special division of soldiers, called the Praetorian Guard, to protect him.
- When Augustus died in 14 CE, his adopted son Tiberius became the next emperor of Rome.

Roman People

Roman society was divided into three main groups of people. There were Roman citizens, non-citizens (or provincials—people who came from outside Rome), and enslaved people. Some provincials and foreigners could become citizens after serving in the Roman army. Enslaved people were not citizens and had no rights.

Roman citizens

At first, only people who had been born in Rome or had Roman parents could be citizens. Citizens could vote and join the army. They had more rights than non-citizens. Later, people from outside Rome were sometimes given citizenship.

Key facts

- The richest Roman citizens were called patricians. They were mostly from the nobility.
- Most Roman citizens were plebeians, or commoners. A plebeian might be a businessman, a shopkeeper, or a poor laborer.
- Citizens also included *equites*, who served in the army and helped run the government.
- Only Roman citizens were allowed to wear a toga—a heavy woolen robe worn in complicated folds.

Enslaved people

Enslaved people were owned by Roman citizens, or by Rome itself. They could be bought and sold. Most were prisoners of war who were brought to Rome as the Romans conquered new lands.

Key facts

- Some enslaved people had cruel masters and were ill-treated; others, especially household slaves, lived well and might even be treated as members of the family.
- Enslaved people owned by the government constructed buildings and bridges or worked in mines. Others were civil servants and helped administer the empire.
- Enslaved people could save money and buy their freedom, or could be freed as a reward for service.
- There were many rebellions by enslaved people. The most famous was led by Spartacus in 73 BCE. He gathered an army of enslaved people, but was defeated in 71 BCE.

The Roman family

Every Roman family was led by a father, called the *paterfamilias*. His household included his wife and children, his sons' wives and their children, and all their property.

Roman woman being dressed by a slave

Key facts

- The *paterfamilias* had absolute power in his household. In theory, he could even condemn his wife, children, servants, or slaves to death.
- Although free-born Roman women were citizens of Rome, they could not vote and did not have the same rights as men.
- During the empire, boys were taught by a tutor at home or they were sent to school.
- Girls did not go to school. Instead, they were taught by their mothers how to run a household.
- Parents chose husbands and wives for their children. Marriages were usually arranged for political or business reasons.

Patricians

Soldier

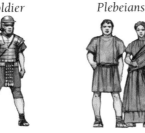
Plebeians

Slaves

Divisions of Roman society

The Roman Army

The Roman army was an outstanding fighting force. It was the army that conquered the empire and kept it together. The army's success was due to discipline, excellent training, and good organization. Army engineers constructed roads, bridges, and buildings to help rule newly conquered lands. The army also helped spread Roman culture throughout the empire.

A Roman legion

In the late 1st century CE, there were 28 Roman legions, or armies. Each legion owned a silver eagle, called an *aquila*, which was carried into battle. If this eagle was captured by the enemy, the whole legion was disbanded in dishonor.

Key facts

- Each legion consisted of around 5,500 men.
- A legion was split into 10 divisions, called cohorts.
- Each cohort was split into smaller units, called centuries.
- A century originally consisted of 100 legionnaires, or foot soldiers. In later years, it contained about 80 legionnaires.
- A legion's silver eagle was carried by a standard-bearer, called the *aquilifer*.

Centurion and legionnaires

Legionnaires

A centurion (right) with two legionnaires

Legionnaires were professional soldiers who were paid to join the Roman army. A legionnaire served in the army for 20–25 years. Only a Roman citizen could become a legionnaire.

Key facts

- The legionnaires in each century were commanded by an officer called a centurion.
- The century's standard-bearer was called the *signifer*.
- Legionnaires were builders as well as fighters. They built roads, forts, and bridges.
- As the best soldiers in the Roman army, legionnaires were mainly used to conquer foreign countries and stamp out rebellions.

Auxiliaries

Every legion was supported by auxiliary soldiers. Auxiliaries were originally recruited from conquered peoples throughout the empire. They were not Roman citizens, but they could receive Roman citizenship after they had finished their period of service in the army.

Key facts

- Auxiliaries were organized into cohorts.
- Each auxiliary cohort contained 500–1,000 men.
- Auxiliaries were used to patrol the frontiers of the Roman Empire, such as Hadrian's Wall in Britain.
- Many auxiliaries served in the cavalry (soldiers who fought on horseback).
- The auxiliary cavalry were highly paid because they had to buy their own horses.
- Most auxiliary cavalry came from Gaul (France and surrounding areas) and Thrace (Bulgaria).

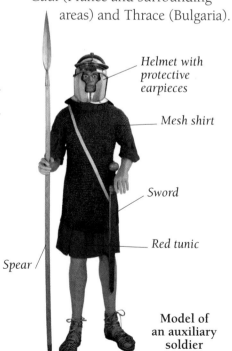

Helmet with protective earpieces

Mesh shirt

Sword

Red tunic

Spear

Model of an auxiliary soldier

Roman Religion

Like the ancient Greeks, the Romans worshiped many different gods. They believed that the gods watched over every part of their lives. The most powerful was Jupiter, the god of the sky and the special protector of the Roman Empire. His statue stood in a great temple on top of the Capitoline Hill in Rome.

Temples

The Romans built temples to honor (show respect for) all the main gods. People made offerings and prayed at temples to ask the gods for help, or to thank them for good fortune in their lives.

Key facts

- The design of Roman temples was based on Etruscan and Greek temples.
- Each temple contained a statue of the god it was built to honor.
- Ceremonies and sacrifices usually took place on an altar outside, at the front of the temple.
- Every family had their own miniature temple, or shrine, in their home, to honor the *lares*—household gods who protected the home and family.

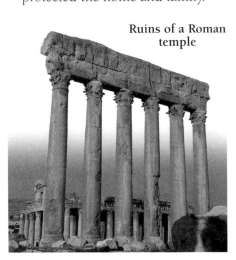

Ruins of a Roman temple

Sacrifices

People sacrificed food, drink, and animals on temple altars to honor the gods. Sacrifices were usually burned so the rising smoke could carry them from this world to the world of the gods.

Sacrificial knife

Key facts

- Animals that were sacrificed included oxen, sheep, goats, pigs, chickens, and doves.
- Certain animals were sacrificed to certain gods. For example, Mercury's "holy animals" were the cock and the ram.
- Male animals were sacrificed to honor gods, and female animals to honor goddesses.
- Only priests conducted sacrifices because Romans believed that, if a sacrifice was not done correctly, the gods might not accept it.

Gods and goddesses

Everyone in the Roman Empire was expected to make offerings to the most important Roman gods. Most emperors were also declared gods after they died, and temples were built to worship them.

Key gods

- Jupiter, king of the gods and sky, protector of the Roman Empire
- Juno, wife of Jupiter and goddess of women
- Mars, god of war
- Neptune, god of the sea
- Diana, goddess of the moon and hunting
- Apollo, god of the sun, healing, and music
- Venus, goddess of love and beauty
- Mercury, messenger of the gods
- Minerva, goddess of crafts and war
- Vesta, goddess of the home
- Ceres, goddess of agriculture
- Vulcan, god of craftsmen and forges
- Roma, goddess of Rome

Jupiter, king of the gods

Master Builders

The Romans were skilled engineers and builders. They constructed thousands of temples, theaters, bridges, aqueducts (bridges to carry water), and roads throughout the empire. Many were built of stone, brick, marble, and a kind of concrete, and are still standing today.

Roman roads

The Romans built a vast network of roads that crisscrossed their empire. The roads were usually built by the Roman army. They were as straight, wide, and smooth as possible, so people could travel easily and quickly. The roads were used by government officials and merchants, as well as the army.

Key facts

- Many Roman roads were so well built that they have survived right up to the present day.
- The surface of a road was gently curved, so that rainwater ran off into ditches at the sides.
- Roman troops had priority on the roads, and everyone else had to give way to them.
- A cohort or legion could march up to 30 miles (50 km) a day on a well-built Roman road.

Aqueducts

Roman engineers cut channels into rocky hillsides to bring water from natural springs in the mountains down to the towns and cities. Where the water had to cross a valley, they built an aqueduct, or water bridge.

Roman aqueduct in Segovia, Spain

Key facts

- An aqueduct had a gentle slope so the water flowed downhill.
- Roman engineers used a plumb line (a weight on a string) to keep walls straight and surfaces level.
- To measure distances, they used long measuring rods and chains.

Domes

The Romans invented the domed roof by crossing a series of arches over each other. Their domes were largely built out of concrete, molded (or cast) into shape around a wooden frame. The most famous dome is that of the Pantheon temple in Rome.

Key facts

- The Romans had invented concrete in the 3rd century BCE. It was the perfect material for building domes because it was strong, yet lighter than stone, and could be molded into shape.
- Roman concrete was made out of rubble, burned limestone, volcanic ash, and water.
- The Pantheon temple was begun by the emperor Hadrian and completed in 128 CE.
- The dome is 141 ft (43 m) wide.
- The temple was dedicated to all the Roman gods.
- The Pantheon has the oldest dome still in existence.

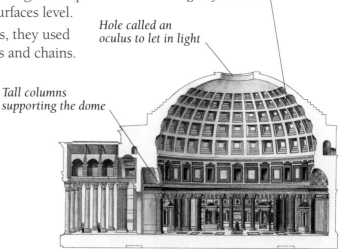

Concrete cast with hollow panels to reduce the weight of the dome

Hole called an oculus to let in light

Tall columns supporting the dome

Cross-section through the Pantheon

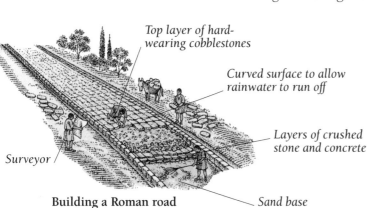

Top layer of hard-wearing cobblestones

Curved surface to allow rainwater to run off

Layers of crushed stone and concrete

Surveyor

Building a Roman road

Sand base

Roman Towns

Towns throughout the Roman empire were all planned in the same way. Public buildings stood in the center of town, arranged around a square called a forum. Homes belonging to wealthy citizens often had heating systems and water supplies. Poorer families usually lived in apartments built above shops and workshops.

The forum

The forum was an open space at the heart of any Roman town or city. It was usually built where the town's two main streets crossed. It was here that markets were held, people met friends, and leaders held ceremonies or victory parades.

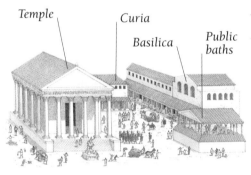

Temple   Curia   Basilica   Public baths

Roman forum

Key facts

- The town's main temple, *basilica* (law court), and *curia* (town hall) were usually built close to the forum.
- A large forum often contained a *rostrum*—a platform used for public speaking and ceremonies.
- Two or three sides of the forum were often surrounded by covered walkways.
- The walkways contained offices, and stalls selling goods.
- A statue of the town's patron god usually stood in the forum.

Roman theaters

Large Roman towns often contained a round amphitheater where people could go and watch public sports and shows, called *ludi* (games). Many towns also had semi-circular theaters, called auditoria (single auditorium), where people could watch plays.

Key facts

- Seats were arranged in tiers so all the spectators had a good view.
- The best seats near the stage were reserved for important citizens. Poorer people sat higher up and farther back.
- People often took along cushions to make the stone seats more comfortable.
- Canvas covers were stretched from poles over the top seats, to keep the sun off the spectators.

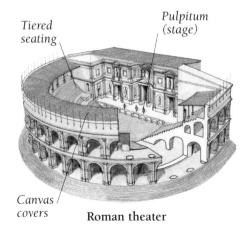

Tiered seating   Pulpitum (stage)

Canvas covers   **Roman theater**

Roman baths

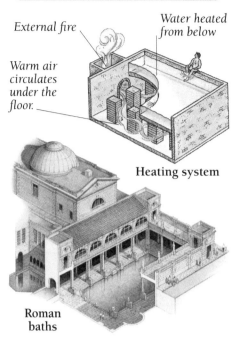

External fire   Water heated from below

Warm air circulates under the floor.

Heating system

Roman baths

Even the smallest, most remote Roman town on the edge of the empire usually had a public bathhouse. The bathhouse was a place to meet friends, relax, do business, or exercise—as well as keep clean.

Key facts

- Roman baths had a series of progressively hotter rooms. The first was a large, cold swimming pool, called the *frigidarium*.
- Next came the *tepidarium*—a warm room with a small pool.
- Last was the *caldarium*—a hot, steamy room with a bathing pool.
- The heat cleaned the pores of the skin through sweating. Dirt and sweat were scraped off the skin with a curved tool called a *strigil*.
- When they were clean, bathers would plunge into a cold-water pool to close their pores.
- Women usually had separate baths, or visited the baths at different times of day from men.

Key dates in ancient Rome

The civilization of ancient Rome began with the building of the city of Rome around 750 BCE. and ended in 476 CE when the last emperor, Romulus Augustulus, was overthrown by a German leader called Odoacer. The Roman Empire in the East, called the Byzantine Empire, continued until it fell to the Turks in 1453.

Finish the timeline

Fill in the missing dates in the timeline, which charts important events in Rome's history. Choose from the dates below, using the information on pages 6–9 to help you.

- 476 CE
- 48 BCE
- 324 CE
- 753 BCE
- 43 CE
- 27 BCE
- 509 BCE
- 146 BCE
- 117 CE
- 264 BCE

Romulus and Remus, legendary founders of Rome

Two consuls, leaders of the senate

....	509 BCE	....	450 BCE	280–272 BCE	....
City of Rome is founded.	Etruscan king Tarquin the Proud is overthrown.	Rome becomes a republic, ruled by the senate	A list of laws, the Twelve Tablets, is published.	The Pyrrhic Wars are fought against King Pyrrhus of Greece.	Rome controls all of Italy. The Punic Wars begin.

Julius Caesar

Coin showing Emperor Augustus

Roman army

....	44 BCE	....	c. 5 BCE–1 CE	14 CE	....
Julius Caesar becomes the ruler of Rome.	Julius Caesar is murdered.	Augustus becomes the first emperor of Rome.	Jesus is born in Palestine, in the Roman Empire.	Death of Augustus. Tiberius becomes emperor.	The Romans invade Britain.

Pantheon

Roman soldier at war

Emperor Constantine

128 CE	161 CE	270 CE	235–284 CE	284 CE	....
The Pantheon temple is completed in Rome.	Emperor Marcus Aurelius fights off attacks from barbarians—tribes outside the empire.	Rome begins to abandon parts of the empire.	Civil wars rage throughout the empire.	Emperor Diocletian divides the empire in two—east and west.	Emperor Constantine briefly reunites the empire.

Color the map

Color in the area ruled by Rome when the empire was at its height in 117 CE, using the map on page 7 as a guide. Add a dot and a label for Rome.

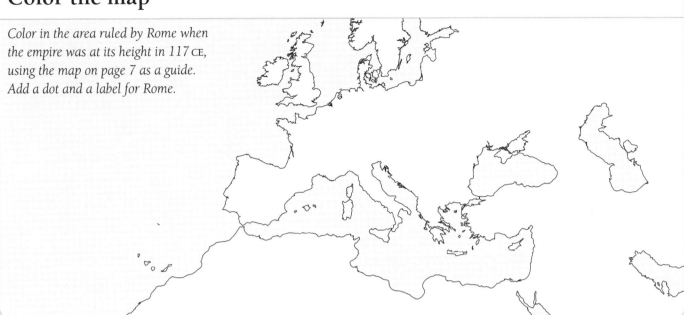

218 BCE
Carthaginian general Hannibal invades Italy.

....
Punic Wars end with defeat of the people of Carthage.

133–31 BCE
Roman rule spreads across Mediterranean.

73–71 BCE
Spartacus leads a rebellion of slaves.

58–50 BCE
Julius Caesar conquers most of Gaul (France and surrounding areas) during Gallic Wars.

Colosseum amphitheater

Trajan's column

Hadrian's Wall

64 CE
A fire destroys large areas of Rome.

69 CE
Emperor Vespasian orders the building of the Colosseum in Rome.

79 CE
Mount Vesuvius erupts, burying the towns of Pompeii and Herculaneum.

113 CE
Trajan column is built in Rome to celebrate Emperor Trajan's wars against Dacia (modern-day Romania).

....
The Roman Empire is at its height.

122 CE
The Romans began to build Hadrian's Wall in Britain to keep out barbarian tribes.

Huns

Invading barbarians

376 CE
The Huns, a fierce Asian tribe, start to force barbarians onto Roman land.

410 CE
A barbarian tribe called the Visigoths captures and sacks (loots) Rome.

455 CE
Rome is sacked again, by a barbarian tribe called the Vandals.

....
Romulus Augustulus loses power. End of empire in the West.

Did you know?

In 79 CE, the volcano Mount Vesuvius erupted, burying the town of Herculaneum under 65 ft (20 m) of ash and debris.

The City of Rome

Over a few hundred years, Rome grew from a small hilltop settlement into the largest, most magnificent city in the ancient world. Emperors commissioned public buildings, such as temples, theaters, and bathhouses, to show off the empire's great power and wealth. There were fountains for drinking water, and beautiful marble statues decorating the main streets and meeting places.

Emperor Augustus rebuilt Rome into a refined city

Label the map of Rome

Finish labeling the important landmarks on this map of Rome according to the descriptions given in the box below.

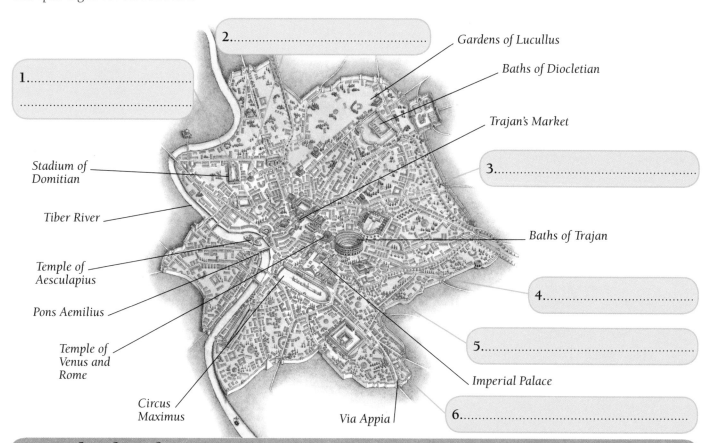

1. ....

2. ....

Gardens of Lucullus

Baths of Diocletian

Trajan's Market

3. ....

Stadium of Domitian

Tiber River

Baths of Trajan

Temple of Aesculapius

Pons Aemilius

4. ....

Temple of Venus and Rome

5. ....

Imperial Palace

Circus Maximus

Via Appia

6. ....

Rome landmarks

Aurelian Wall Wall built around the whole city of Rome, completed in around 280 CE.

Baths of Caracalla Public bathhouse set within a vast walled square. They are situated near the Via Appia.

Colosseum Huge amphitheater (circular building with tiers of seats round an arena), standing next to the Baths of Trajan.

Pantheon Domed temple dedicated to all the Roman gods, situated next to the Stadium of Domitian.

Roman Forum Open space near Trajan's Market, surrounded by public buildings.

Theatre of Marcellus Semicircular theater standing on the banks of the Tiber, opposite the Temple of Aesculapius.

Roman Ruins

Even though the Roman Empire came to an end around 1,500 years ago, Roman engineers and architects were so skilled at constructing huge, strong buildings that many of their buildings are still standing today. These include baths, basilicas (courthouses), bridges, and aqueducts (channels for carrying water into cities).

Ruins of Temple of Jupiter, in Lebanon

Identify the ruin

Identify these ruins of famous Roman structures from the descriptions given in the building facts on the right.

1.......................................

2.......................................

3..

....

4...

Building facts

- The Colosseum, Rome's famous circular amphitheater, was completed in 80 CE.
- The Arch of Septimius Severus was built in Rome in 203 CE to celebrate Emperor Septimius Severus's 10th year of reign.
- The Roman Forum was an open space at the heart of the city of Rome, surrounded by huge public buildings.
- The Aquae Sulis baths at Bath, England, were built around a hot spring.
- Trajan's Market—a kind of huge shopping mall built on several levels—was begun in 107 CE, in Rome.
- The Pont du Gard, a famous aqueduct in southern France, was built around 19 BCE.
- The Pons Aemilius, the first stone bridge to be built across the Tiber River in Rome, was completed in 142 BCE.

When was it built?

Number the following structures to show the order in which they were built, starting with the earliest. Use the dates given on this page and the charts at the back of the book to help you.

 Colosseum   Pont du Gard   The Pantheon

   Trajan's Market   Arch of Septimius Severus   Pons Aemilius

Hail Caesar!

Gaius Julius Caesar (c. 100–44 BCE) was a great military leader and politician who saw victory in war as a way of winning power, wealth, and fame. He became the sole ruler of Rome in 48 BCE, and played a large part in turning the Roman Republic into what was to become the Roman Empire.

Caesar's rise and fall

The following pictures and captions tell the story of Caesar's career. Number them in the correct order, starting with the earliest event. Use the Caesar facts to help you.

Caesar facts

- Caesar was first appointed to the Roman senate in 69 BCE.
- He became governor of Hispania (Spain) in 61 BCE.
- He became part of the First Triumvirate in 60 BCE.
- Caesar started the Gallic Wars (58–50 BCE). He also led two expeditions to Britain (55 and 54 BCE).
- In 49 BCE, Caesar was recalled to Rome, sparking a civil war.
- He defeated Pompey's troops in 48 BCE, becoming sole ruler.
- In 45 BCE, he returned to Rome and was made dictator for life.
- Caesar was stabbed to death in the senate in 44 BCE.

a. Caesar becomes consul and joins forces with two other senators, Pompey and Crassus. The three men rule Rome together, and are known as the First Triumvirate.

b. Caesar is elected Pontifex Maximus (chief priest) of Rome in 63 BCE. Two years later, he becomes governor of Hispania. Caesar rules successfully in Hispania, expanding Roman rule.

c. Caesar is murdered by a group of senators, led by Brutus and Cassius, who want to restore the republic.

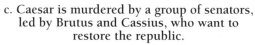

d. Caesar defeats Pompey's troops in Greece and becomes sole ruler. He returns to Rome in triumph in 45 BCE, and holds magnificent parades and feasts to celebrate his victories.

e. Caesar is made governor of part of Gaul (southern France). He starts the Gallic Wars and conquers most of Gaul for Rome.

f. Caesar is ordered back to Rome by the senate, who fears he is becoming too powerful. He leads his troops across the Rubicon River at the northern frontier of Italy, starting a civil war.

g. Caesar starts his political career in 69 BCE, when he is elected quaestor (financial administrator) in the senate. He soon earns a reputation as a good public speaker.

Did you know?

Images of Caesar in later life show him with his hair combed forward to hide his baldness.

h. As dictator of Rome, Caesar makes many reforms. Although his reforms are popular, he acts as if he is a king, without consulting the senate.

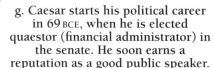

Emperors of Rome

Augustus, the first emperor of Rome, ruled from 27 BCE to 14 CE. His reign began a long period of stability known as the *Pax Romana*, or Roman Peace, which lasted for nearly 200 years. Altogether, the empire had around 95 emperors. During certain periods, two or more men claimed the title of emperor at the same time. At other times, there was no clear emperor at all.

Emperor Hadrian

Mix-and-match emperors

Match each emperor to the correct description. Use the information on the charts at the back of the book to help you.

1. Became the first emperor of Rome and ruled wisely for 41 years.
2. Built a great wall in northern England to protect Roman lands from barbarian tribes.
3. Declared emperor after the death of Caligula in 41 CE; a good orator (public speaker) and historian; ordered the invasion of Britain.
4. This emperor came to power soon after the murder of Nero. He quickly restored order and began many public building projects, including temples and theaters.

Vespasian

Claudius

Augustus

Hadrian

The Roman forum

Name the buildings on this drawing of the Roman Forum in 306 CE, using the descriptions in the box on the left.

Forum buildings

Rostrum A platform holding five pillars topped with eagles, used in victory parades.

Arch of Septimius Severus A large, white marble arch near the Rostrum, erected in 203 CE to celebrate Emperor Septimius Severus's 10th year of reign.

Arch of Augustus An arch beside the Temple of Vesta, built to celebrate Augustus's victory over Mark Antony at the Battle of Actium in 31 BCE.

Temple of Julius Caesar A temple situated opposite the Rostrum and next to the Arch of Augustus, built to honor Julius Caesar.

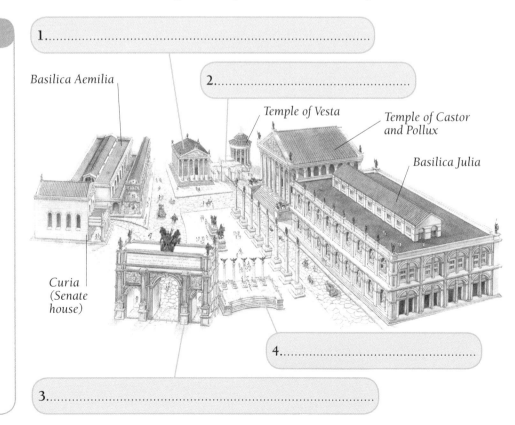

1. ....

2. ....

Basilica Aemilia

Temple of Vesta

Temple of Castor and Pollux

Basilica Julia

Curia (Senate house)

3. ....

4. ....

Trade Across the Empire

During the *Pax Romana*, when the lands around the Mediterranean Sea were at peace, the Roman Empire became rich and prosperous. Merchants carried goods to different parts of the Empire by ship, or on the army's huge network of roads. The Romans imported goods such as glass, metal, and wool. They exported mainly olive oil and wine in tall pottery jars, called *amphorae* (singular *amphora*).

Amphorae were shaped so they could be tightly packed together in a ship's hold.

Where do they come from?

Draw the missing goods brought into Rome from around the empire, to complete the chart.

Goods	Imported from
 Arabian horses  Lions and elephants for gladiator shows	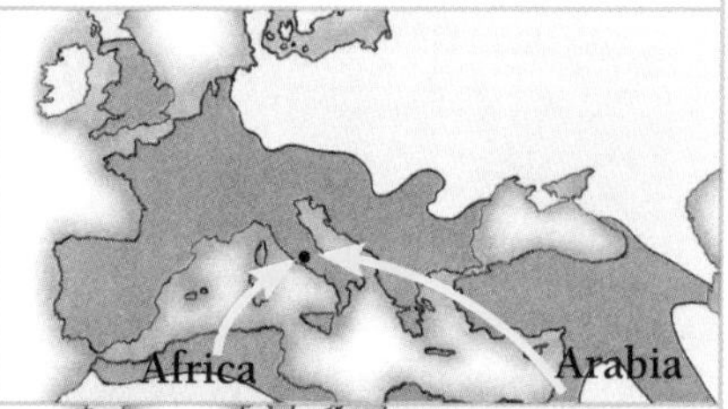
Sheep's wool and cloth 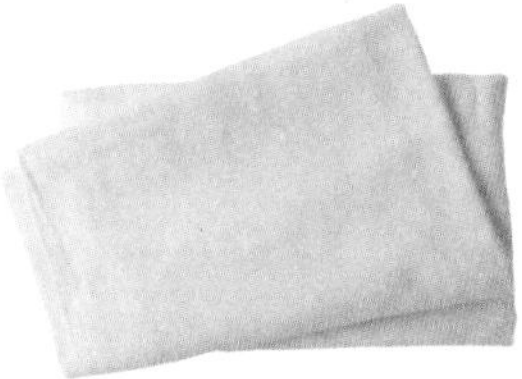	
Glassware 	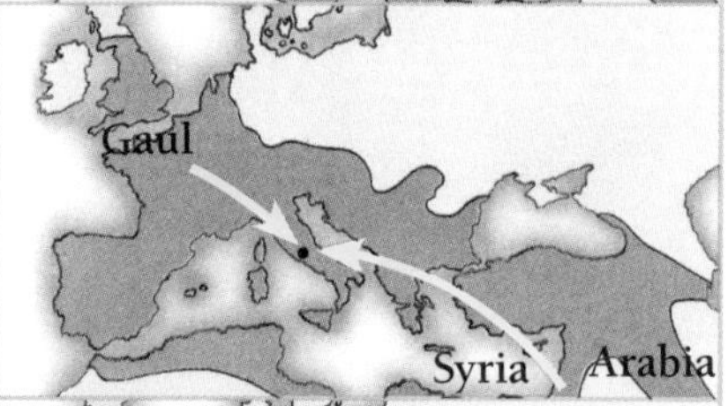
 Fruits such as figs and pomegranates	
Enslaved people 	

Money Matters

As the Romans began to rule more and more land, they became richer. Trade grew and, by the time of the Punic Wars in 264 BCE, the Romans controlled a huge, complicated trading network with banks, moneylenders, and mints that made money.

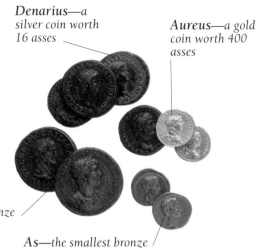

Denarius—a silver coin worth 16 asses

Aureus—a gold coin worth 400 asses

Sestertius—a bronze coin worth 4 asses (plural sestertii)

As—the smallest bronze coin (plural asses)

Shopping list

- Six bunches of grapes
- Two fish
- One sack of peppercorns
- Three sacks of wheat
- Three bunches of mixed herbs
- Ten pottery bowls

Take a shopping trip

Imagine that you are enslaved. You have been sent by your master to buy the things on this shopping list at Trajan's Market in Rome. You have been given one gold aureus (worth 400 asses) to spend.

See how much each item costs below, then figure out how much money you need to spend, and how much change you should get from your aureus.
(Tip: Add up the amounts in asses.)

FISH	SACK OF PEPPERCORNS	BUNCH OF MIXED HERBS	SACK OF WHEAT	GRAPES	BOWL
3 sestertii (12 asses) each	1 sestertius (4 asses) a sack	2 asses	1 denarius (16 asses) a sack	3 asses a bunch	1 denarius (16 asses) each

1. Altogether, I will spend .... at the market.

2. I should get .... change from my gold *aureus*.

Money facts

- The first Roman coins were minted in around 290 BCE.
- The first coin was the as. It was made of bronze.
- Coins had images on them, such as emperors, gods, and important events or buildings.
- When Augustus became the first emperor, he took over control of the different mints, and gave coins a fixed value.
- The aureus was Rome's first gold coin. *Aureus* means golden from the Latin word *aurum*, meaning gold.

A Legionnaire's Life

A Roman legionnaire was strong and tough. Soldiers learned how to march in line, to fight with a sword and javelin, and to build and dismantle camps. Some soldiers were trained as surveyors or engineers. They supervised the building of bridges, roads, and forts.

Packing a load

When on the march, every legionnaire carried a heavy pack over his shoulder. Look carefully at the picture, then check the two items that would not have been carried in a legionnaire's pack.

- Cooking pan
- Dish for food
- A novel
- Leather bottle for water or wine
- Mattock, or pick, for digging ditches
- Gardening fork
- Turf cutter for building ramparts (defensive walls)
- Woolen cloak
- Leather pack containing three days' supply of food

A legionnaire's gear

Look at the pictures and read the descriptions of a legionnaire's armor and weapons. Can you match the caption to the correct picture?

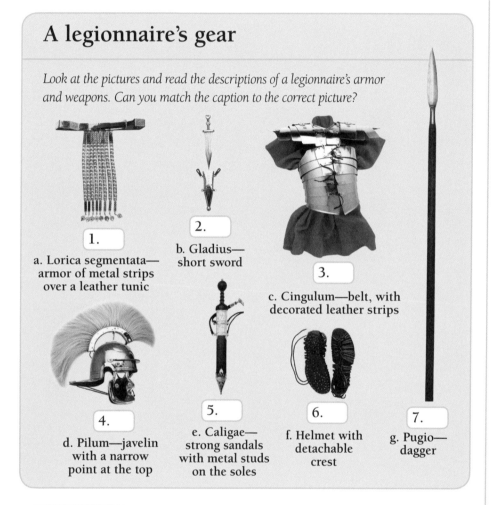

1.

a. Lorica segmentata— armor of metal strips over a leather tunic

2.

b. Gladius— short sword

3.

c. Cingulum—belt, with decorated leather strips

4.

d. Pilum—javelin with a narrow point at the top

5.

e. Caligae— strong sandals with metal studs on the soles

6.

f. Helmet with detachable crest

7.

g. Pugio— dagger

Prepared for battle

Fill in the missing words, using the information in the box above.

1. A legionnaire carried a short, stabbing sword called a ....

2. He also carried a ...., or dagger.

3. His body armor was called a ....

4. His belt, or ...., was worn to protect the groin.

Did you know?

Because of their heavy packs, legionnaires were nicknamed "Marius's mules" after the general who introduced the packs.

Into Battle

The Roman army was highly skilled in battle tactics and attacking a fortified, or walled, town. If a town refused to surrender, the legionnaires built siege towers so they could climb over the walls. They also hammered at the gates with massive battering rams. When attacking, the soldiers marched with their shields over their heads in a defensive formation called a testudo, meaning tortoise.

Siege warfare

Number the following items on the picture of Roman soldiers attacking a fortified town. Use the information in the introduction to help you.

1. Testudo
2. Siege tower
3. Covered battering ram

A Roman Fort

Draw lines to the different parts of this Roman fort.

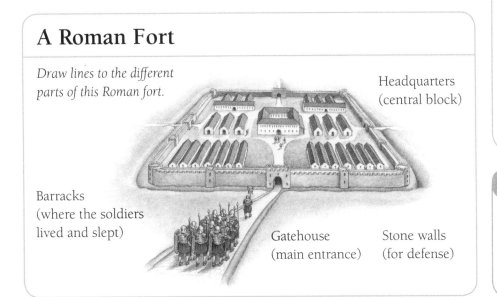

Headquarters (central block)

Barracks (where the soldiers lived and slept)

Gatehouse (main entrance)

Stone walls (for defense)

Did you know?

Siege towers and battering rams were covered with dampened animal skins to stop them being set on fire by the enemy.

Design a standard

Each legion, cohort, and century had its own standard (flag)—its most prized possession. Look at the picture below, then design your own standard in the space provided.

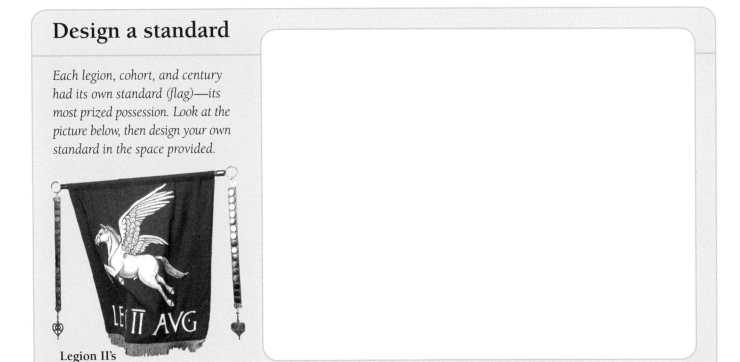

Legion II's Pegasus standard

Roman Homes

In towns, a few wealthy Romans lived in private town houses. Each house, called a *domus*, was surrounded by high walls with few windows. Inside, light, spacious rooms faced a courtyard called an atrium, which was used to receive guests. Some houses had flushing toilets connected to the town's sewers, and (in cold climates) an underfloor heating system called a hypocaust.

Did you know?

Many wealthy Romans had a villa in the country as well as a town house. A few villas were simply places for their owners to relax, away from busy city life, but most were run as farms.

Inside a Roman town house

Read the descriptions of the parts of a Roman town house below, then fill in the labels.

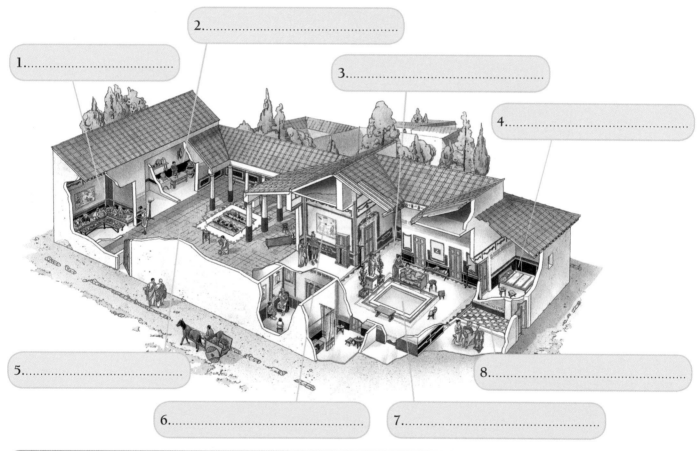

1. ....

2. ....

3. ....

4. ....

5. ....

6. ....

7. ....

8. ....

Parts of a town house

Atrium An open-air courtyard.

Impluvium A pool for collecting rainwater from the sloping roofs.

Triclinium A dining room with couches where guests could recline while eating.

Culina The kitchen, where enslaved people prepared the food.

Peristylium A courtyard surrounded by columns and covered walkways.

Mural A decorative, patterned frieze painted on the walls.

Cubiculum A bedroom, where people slept on low beds or couches.

Mosaic floor Flooring made up of thousands of tiny ceramic tiles, called *tesserae*, arranged to form a picture or pattern.

How a hypocaust works

Look at this drawing of how a hypocaust system works, then write numbers in the boxes to put the four stages in the correct order.

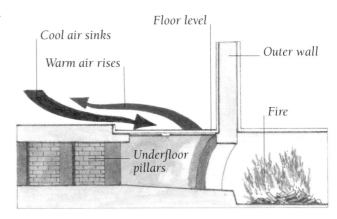

Cross-section of a hypocaust

- ☐ The floor heats up and causes warm air to rise into the room above.

- ☐ A fire is lit below an outer wall.

- ☐ Cooler air sinks and is warmed by the floor.

- ☐ Heat from the fire warms the air around a series of underfloor pillars.

Apartment living

Most people, especially in large cities such as Rome itself, lived in huge, overcrowded apartment blocks, called *insulae* (singular *insula*). On the ground floor were shops and workshops. The four or five floors above were divided into apartments. Richer people might have several rooms on a lower floor. Poorer families crammed into tiny rooms on the upper floors. Many *insulae* were badly built and they sometimes collapsed.

A typical Roman apartment block

Apartment facts

- Waste was thrown out of the windows into the street.
- Fresh water had to be fetched in jars from public fountains.
- The lower floors were often built of stone, and the upper floors of wood.
- Most apartment buildings had no toilets, so people used chamber pots or public toilets in the street, called *foricae*.
- People used woodburning braziers (small stoves) to keep their rooms warm.
- There were no chimneys, so fire was a constant risk.

Read the information on this page about apartment living, then answer the questions below.

1. What were apartment blocks called?

....

2. How many floors high were they?

....

3. What were *foricae*?

....

4. Did richer people live on the higher or lower floors?

....

5. Give two reasons why there was a risk of fire.

....

....

Roman art

The Romans loved beautiful things. They made fine pottery, delicate jewelery, colorful mosaics, and murals (wall paintings). They also made stone carvings called reliefs, in which the picture stood out from its background. Romans were especially skilled at glass-making, and sometimes used a technique called cameo carving. This involved covering dark glass with a layer of white glass. The white layer was then carved to form a picture and reveal the dark color underneath.

A Roman cameo vase

Pictures in stone

This picture shows a section of Trajan's column in Rome. It is covered in relief carving, showing scenes from Emperor Trajan's military victories. Draw lines from the descriptions to match the correct parts in the picture,

Roman legionnaires building a fort

Roman legionnaires carrying shields and marching out of a gateway

Roman boats tied together to form a bridge across the river

River god protecting the Romans' boats

Art puzzle

Draw a line to match the type of art to its description, using the information on this page and page 27.

1. A picture made using lots of tiny cubes of colored glass or stone.
2. A kind of sculpture in which the carved picture stands out from the background.
3. A relief carving on glass or a gemstone in which the picture is a different color from the background.
4. A large design or picture painted onto a wall.

Cameo

Mosaic

Mural

Relief

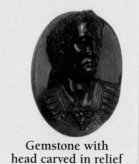

Gemstone with head carved in relief

Mosaics

The walls and floors of many Roman buildings were richly decorated with mosaics made using tiny cubes of pottery, glass, or stone such as marble. The tiny cubes, called *tesserae* (singular *tessera*), were placed in position on wet plaster to form a picture or a pattern.

Finish the mosaic

Draw dark tesserae *inside the outlines to complete this mosaic picture of a dog, which was found in the ruins of Pompeii—a town near Mount Vesuvius in Italy.*

Make a mosaic

Follow these steps to make your own mosaic. You will need plain white cardboard, colored paper or magazines, scissors, and glue.

1 First, plan your design on a spare sheet of paper. Then, using a pencil, neatly copy your design onto the white cardboard.

2 Cut out lots of tiny squares from colored paper or magazines. Each piece should measure about ³⁄₈ in (1.5 cm) square.

3 Glue the squares in neat rows onto the cardboard, following your design.

Mosaic mix-up

These pictures and captions show four stages in making a mosaic. Number the stages 1 to 4, to put them in the right order.

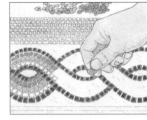

a.

The *tesserae* were pressed into the still-damp plaster, in neat rows.

b.

The surface being worked on was thinly spread with plaster, a small area at a time.

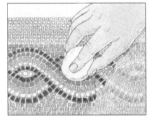

c.

The gaps between the tiles were filled with plaster. Once dry, the *tesserae* were polished.

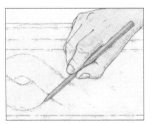

d.

The pattern being created was drawn onto the wet plaster using a pointed tool.

Roman Fashion

Early Roman clothing was modeled on the flowing robes worn by the ancient Greeks. Men wore a robe called a toga—a piece of woolen fabric worn in folds and draped around the body. Women wore a longer robe called a stola and a shawl called a palla. Enslaved people wore simple, short tunics tied at the waist.

Did you know?

Purple dye was very expensive and few people were allowed to wear this color. Senators wore togas with a purple band around the hem. Victorious generals and, later, emperors wore purple togas edged in gold.

Fashion labels

Label these pictures of people in Roman dress, using the information on this page:
Choose from: **stola   tunic   palla   toga   leather sandals**

1..........................

2..........................

3..........................

5..................

4..............................

Beauty facts

Roman women sometimes:

- wore blush and lipstick made from wine dregs.
- used bear fat mixed with soot to blacken their eyebrows.
- had their ears pierced for earrings.
- whitened their faces with powdered chalk or white lead.
- curled their hair with heated tongs.
- wore elaborate, braided hairpieces.

Braided hairpiece

Sandal styles

In the early days of the Republic, many Romans were barefoot at home or wore simple, soft sandals. Outdoors, they might wear heavier sandals or boots. Later, shoemakers became skilled at making different styles of sandal out of leather and canvas.

Read the descriptions and match the captions to the correct picture.

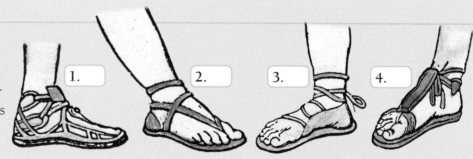

1.   2.   3.   4.

a. Simple sandal with thong between the toes

b. Sandal tying in front of ankle

c. Elegant ladies' sandal with ornate leather strap

d. Sandals with leather sides and heel, and ankle straps

Make a Roman toga

Follow these steps to make yourself a Roman toga.

1 Cut out a piece of fabric into a semicircle. (Try using two old sheets sewn together.)

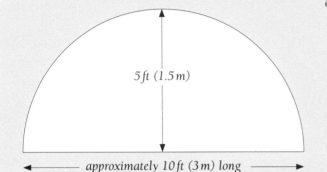

5 ft (1.5 m)

← approximately 10 ft (3 m) long →

2 Drape one end of the fabric over your left shoulder, holding the free end in your right hand.

3 Fold over the top part of the right section and roll the folded edge over two or three times.

4 Now throw the bottom of the free right edge over your left shoulder.

5 Tuck part of the loose looped fabric into the front of your belt, to secure it.

2.

3.

4.

5.

Grooming facts

In the early days of the Roman Republic, many men wore beards. But, from around 300 BCE, it became fashionable to be clean-shaven. Barbershops sprung up all over Rome so men could have a daily shave. Hadrian, who ruled from 117 CE, became the first emperor to wear a beard (possibly to cover a scar on his face). After this, wearing beards became fashionable again.

Most Roman men wore their hair short, and were clean-shaven.

Beards became popular during the reign of Emperor Hadrian.

Did you know?

In the 2nd century CE, the Romans began the custom of wearing wedding rings on the third finger of the left hand. They believed a nerve ran from that finger straight to the heart.

Fashion quiz

Circle the correct word to complete the following sentences, using the information given on this page and the page opposite.

1. Women blackened their eyebrows with   **soot / chalk / wine dregs**

2. Enslaved people usually wore   **togas / tunics / pallas**

3. Augustus / Hadrian / Constantine   was the first emperor to wear a beard

4. Senators wore togas with a   **gold / purple / white**   hem band

5. The Romans invented the custom of wearing   **beards / sandals / wedding rings**

Food and drink

The Romans rose early and started the day with a simple breakfast of bread or wheat cakes, with honey, olives, or dates. Lunch, called *prandium*, was similar. However, most Romans skipped lunch and waited for *cena* – the main meal of the day. This usually started at three in the afternoon. Poorer people mostly ate bread with a few vegetables or eggs or perhaps some sausage. Wealthier people also ate fruit, fish, and meat. The most common drink was wine mixed with water.

Bread

Did you know?

Poorer people did not have kitchens, so they bought hot food from taverns or from *thermopolia* (bars) selling hot drinks and snacks.

Inside a Roman kitchen

This picture shows a reconstruction of a Roman kitchen. Read the descriptions below of various objects used in the kitchen, then find and number the objects in the picture.

a.
b.
c.
d.
e.
f.
g.

Kitchen facts

1. Most of the cooking was done in pots standing on metal gridirons or racks on a **raised brick hearth**.

2. **Metal frying pans** were hung up by their handles when not in use.

3. **Strings of onions and dried herbs** hung from the walls and ceilings.

4. **Baskets** were used to store vegetables and fruit.

5. Wine was bought and stored in two-handled jars called *amphorae*. They had pointed bases that had to be leaned against the wall.

6. Round *amphorae* contained olive oil used in cooking.

7. Food was prepared on a **wooden table**.

A Roman Feast

In wealthy households, *cena* was a social event as well as a leisurely meal. There were often guests, with entertainment from dancers, jugglers, and clowns between courses. People ate while reclining on low couches that each held up to three people. The couches were placed around three sides of a low table. The fourth side was left open so that enslaved people had room to serve the family and their guests.

Banquet menu

Name the foods pictured on this menu for a Roman banquet.

APPETIZERS
Olives • Radish salad
• Mushrooms • Eggs
• Oysters • Milk-fed snails

MAIN COURSE
Sea bream • Hot Boiled Goose
• Stuffed Hare
• Lentils with Chestnuts
• Songbirds with Asparagus and Quail's Eggs • Lettuce Leaves with Onions • Truffles

DESSERT
Fresh Figs • Stuffed Dates
• Grapes • Honey Cakes

Roman food puzzle

Take a look at this list, then put a tick beside four things that the ancient Romans did NOT eat. Use the menu above as a guide.

Nuts	☐	Lentils	☐
Tomatoes	☐	Oranges	☐
Pasta	☐	Figs	☐
Lettuce	☐	Bananas	☐

Did you know?

Dormice were a popular delicacy. They were kept in straw-filled earthenware pots, where they were fattened up on chestnuts, walnuts, and acorns. One recipe involved cooking dormice in honey with poppy seeds.

Sweet treats

Try making this Roman recipe for stuffed dates.

You will need:
• 6 dates per person
• A handful of shelled almonds, hazelnuts, or pine nuts
• Pepper
• Salt
• 3 tablespoons (50ml) honey

1 Take the pits out of the dates.

2 Stuff the dates with the nuts (at least one of each type per date) and add a pinch of pepper.

3 Roll the dates in a little salt.

4 Heat the honey in a frying pan, quickly fry the dates*, then serve immediately.

* WARNING: Ask an adult for help when using the stove

Roman Writing

Many different languages were spoken across the Roman Empire but Latin was the main language used for trade, government, and communication. The Romans brought writing to northern Europe, and the Latin alphabet is still widely used today. The Romans, however, only had 22 letters in their alphabet—J, U, W, and Y did not exist.

Roman writing at a desk

A B C D E F G
H I K L M N O P
Q R S T V X Z

Roman writing

Try writing the following in Latin capital letters. Use an "I" for "J" and a "V" for "U" or "W". Leave out the letter "Y."

Your name: ....

Your address: ....

....

Writing facts

- The Romans wrote on waxed tablets with a metal pen called a stylus. They also wrote on Egyptian papyrus (paper made from reeds) using a reed pen and ink.
- Pieces of papyrus were glued together to form a long sheet, which was rolled into a scroll.
- The finest books were written on long-lasting vellum, made from wafer-thin animal skin.
- Ink for writing on wood, papyrus, or vellum was made of fine soot mixed with water.
- During late Roman times, the Romans invented a kind of book with pages, called a *codex*.

True or false?

Check the boxes to show which of these statements are true or false, using the information on this page to help you.

	TRUE	FALSE
1. Ink was used for writing on papyrus.	☐	☐
2. There was no letter "V" in the Roman alphabet.	☐	☐
3. The Romans wrote on waxed tablets with a reed pen.	☐	☐
4. Vellum was made from animal skin.	☐	☐

Roman writing materials

Roman Numbers

Roman numerals were written using a combination of seven letters: "I" for 1, "V" for 5, and so on. Any number placed after a similar-sized or larger number was added on. For example, II (1+1) was 2, and VI (5+1) was 6. However, where a smaller number was placed *before* a larger one, the smaller number was *subtracted* from the larger one. For example IV (5-1) was 4, IX (10–1) was 9.

Did you know?

Today, some clocks and watches have Roman numerals on the clockface.

Number facts

I	1	XXX	30
II	2	XL	40
III	3	L	50
IV	4	LX	60
V	5	LXX	70
VI	6	LXXX	80
VII	7	XC	90
VIII	8	C	100
IX	9	D	500
X	10	M	1,000
XII	12	MM	2,000
XX	20	MMM	3,000

Number puzzle

Try to write the following in Roman numerals, using the information on the scroll on the left to help you.

1. Your age ....

2. Your telephone number, using a Roman numeral for each digit (ignore zero since the Romans did not use this number)

....

3. Today's date, using a number for the month ....

4. Your date of birth ....

5. The number 555 in Roman numerals* ....

* Tip: Put the numbers in order, from largest to smallest.

Centum puzzle

A centipede

In Latin, the word for 100 is centum. *The following words are based on the Latin word for 100. Can you match them up to their meanings?*

Centurion

1. Century   a. Leader of 100 men in the Roman army

2. Centurion   b. There are 100 of these in one dollar

3. Centimeter   c. Animal with (about) 100 legs

4. Cent   d. 100 years

5. Centipede   e. $\frac{1}{100}$th part of a meter

A centurion with his troops

Entertainment

There were big differences between the lives of the rich and the poor. Yet all Romans could share certain pleasures of city life, such as a visit to the racetrack, a long soak in a bathhouse, or a trip to the theater to see a play. The Romans also enjoyed board games and gambling with coins and dice.

Chariot racing

Racing facts

- Up to 24 chariot races took place in a single day.
- In each race, there were usually 12 chariots racing for 7 laps—a total of about 5 miles (8 km).
- There were four teams, each with a different color—reds, blues, greens, and whites.
- Each chariot was usually pulled by two or four horses.
- In special races, charioteers raced with six or eight horses to each chariot.

Play knucklebones

Here is how you can play knucklebones—a game once enjoyed by Roman children, using bones from a pig's or sheep's foot.

Shape four bones from self-hardening modeling clay. Write or carve the Roman numbers I, V, X, and L (for 1, 5, 10, and 50) on each of the long sides.

How to play the game:

1 Take turns to throw the "bones" on the ground.

2 Count the number of points from each throw, based on the Roman numerals that land face up.

3 Award extra points for any of the following different combinations:
Four of a kind = C (100) points
Three of a kind = L (50) points
Two of a kind = V (5 points)

4 Anyone who throws four Is in one try is out of the game.
Anyone who throws a I, V, X, and L in one try wins the game.
Otherwise, the first player to reach M (1,000) points is the winner.

Racing at the Circus Maximus

Read the racing facts above then circle the correct words in the following sentences:

1. There were **four / six / eight** teams of charioteers.

2. A race covered **three / five / seven** laps.

3. Every race usually had **8 / 12 / 24** chariots taking part.

4. There were often **8 / 12 / 24** races a day.

Gladiator Fights

One of the most popular pastimes in ancient Rome was going to watch trained fighters called gladiators fight to the death. These games were usually paid for by the emperors and other important Romans, who wanted to win popularity with the people.

At the Colosseum

Read the facts about the Colosseum, Rome's most famous amphitheater. Then number the parts of the picture to match the facts below.

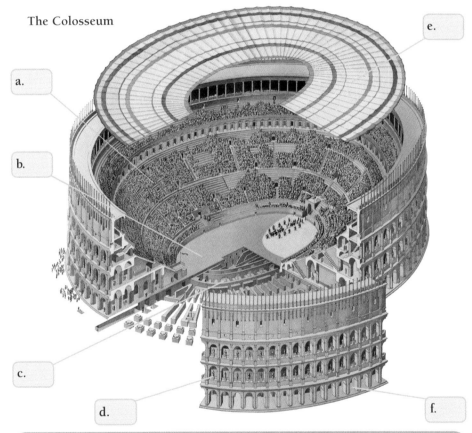

The Colosseum

a.

b.

c.

d.

e.

f.

Colosseum facts

1. There were 80 **entrances** to the Colosseum, so that people could enter and leave quickly.

2. **Statues** of famous Romans and Roman gods decorated the outside of the amphitheater.

3. The Colosseum provided **tiered seating** for 50,000 spectators.

4. A maze of **underground rooms** below the arena was used for storage or caged animals.

5. The **arena floor** was covered with sand to soak up spilled blood.

6. **Canvas covers** were stretched over wooden posts to shelter spectators from the sun.

Gladiator types

Number the four types of gladiators according to their descriptions.

1. The **secutor** carried a huge shield and a sword.

2. The **hoplomachus** had a spear, sword, and shield and wore protective leg and arm coverings.

3. The **retiarius** fought with a net and a three-pronged spear called a trident.

4. The **murmillo** ("fish man") wore a helmet with a high crest like a fish's fin. He carried a short sword and a round shield.

a.

b.

c.

d.

Gods and Goddesses

Across the Roman Empire, people worshiped hundreds of different gods and goddesses. Everyone, however, was expected to make sacrifices to the most important Roman gods, such as Jupiter. They also prayed to past emperors, who were often worshiped as gods after they had died.

Who's who?

Answer the following questions, using the information on page 11 to help you.

1. Who was the Romans' most powerful god?

....

2. Who was the goddess of the moon and hunting?

....

3. Name the goddess of Rome. ....

4. Whose temple designs did the Romans copy?

....

5. Who was the messenger of the gods?

....

6. Name Jupiter's wife. ....

Praying for help

Using the information on page 11, which god or goddess do you think a Roman would pray to if he or she:

1. was unlucky in love.

....

2. wanted a good harvest.

....

3. wanted to be cured of an illness.

....

4. had to travel by ship.

....

5. hoped to fight well in a battle.

....

and ....

Proserpina, daughter of Ceres

Christianity facts

Some Romans lost faith in their state religion and began to follow the teachings of Jesus of Nazareth (born c. 5 BCE). They called themselves Christians and followed only one god, refusing to make offerings to the Roman gods. As a result, they were ill-treated and even killed. Even so, the religion spread throughout the empire and beyond.

• The earliest Christian symbols were a cross and a fish.

Priests and Sacrifice

The Latin word for priest was *pontifex*, and the chief priest of Rome was called the *Pontifex Maximus*. In the days of the Republic, this was an elected position. Later, emperors automatically became Rome's chief priest.

Sacrifice puzzle

Use the information on this page and on page 11 to answer the following questions.

1. What was the Latin name for the chief priest of Rome?

....

2. Where were sacrifices made?

....

3. Name three types of animal that were offered as sacrifices.

....

....

4. Which animal organ was believed to carry messages?

....

5. Which priests read messages from the gods in natural signs, such as cloud patterns?

....

Priest facts

- The *Pontifex Maximus* performed ceremonies in honor of the gods. These included prayers, the burning of incense, and sacrificing animals as gifts for the gods.
- Roman priests called *haruspices* studied the insides of sacrificed animals.
- The Romans believed that the shape and condition of an animal's liver revealed messages from the gods.
- Before he sacrificed an animal, a priest sprinkled cornmeal or wine on the animal's head.
- Priests called *augurs* observed thunder and lightning, and studied unusual patterns made by birds, clouds, or stars, to discover the will of the gods.

Making a sacrifice

Number the following parts on this picture of a Roman woman with a priest making a sacrifice to the gods.

1. Libation (drink offering, such as milk or wine) being poured onto the fire
2. Priest
3. Priest's staff
4. Libation jug
5. Altar

Sacrificing a boar

37

History of Ancient Rome

Check or number the boxes to answer each question. Check your answers on page 46.

1 According to legend, Rome was founded by:

- ☐ **a.** Saturn
- ☐ **b.** Jupiter
- ☐ **c.** Romulus and Remus
- ☐ **d.** Roma, goddess of Rome

2 Which two groups of people influenced early Rome?

- ☐ **a.** Britons
- ☐ **b.** Etruscans
- ☐ **c.** Greeks
- ☐ **d.** Germanic tribes

3 The Romans defeated the Greeks in the:

- ☐ **a.** Punic Wars
- ☐ **b.** Etruscan Wars
- ☐ **c.** Gallic Wars
- ☐ **d.** Pyrrhic Wars

4 Hannibal was a famous:

- ☐ **a.** Carthaginian general
- ☐ **b.** Greek warlord
- ☐ **c.** Etruscan king
- ☐ **d.** Roman consul

5 Number steps 1–5, in the order in which they happened.

- ☐ **a.** The Romans defeated the Carthaginians.
- ☐ **b.** The Romans defeated the Etruscans.
- ☐ **c.** The city of Rome was founded.
- ☐ **d.** The Romans defeated the Greeks.
- ☐ **e.** The Romans invaded Gaul.

6 The Roman Empire was at its height in:

- ☐ **a.** 475 CE
- ☐ **b.** 44 BCE
- ☐ **c.** 117 CE
- ☐ **d.** 27 BCE

7 The Roman civilization in the west lasted around:

- ☐ **a.** 550 years
- ☐ **b.** 1,200 years
- ☐ **c.** 2,500 years
- ☐ **d.** 4,000 years

8 When did Rome became a republic?

- ☐ **a.** 27 BCE
- ☐ **b.** 753 BCE
- ☐ **c.** 44 BCE
- ☐ **d.** 509 BCE

9 Which of the following was *not* built in the city of Rome?

- ☐ **a.** Pantheon
- ☐ **b.** Colosseum
- ☐ **c.** Pont du Gard
- ☐ **d.** Baths of Caracalla
- ☐ **e.** Circus Maximus

10 The *Pax Romana* (Roman Peace) lasted for:

- ☐ **a.** 1,000 years
- ☐ **b.** 100 years
- ☐ **c.** 200 years
- ☐ **d.** 2,000 years

11 The Roman Empire in the west ended in:

- ☐ **a.** 476 CE
- ☐ **b.** 284 CE
- ☐ **c.** 270 CE
- ☐ **d.** 330 CE

Rulers and Citizens

Check or number the boxes to answer each question. Check your answers on page 46.

1 During the Republic, Rome was ruled by:

- a. kings
- b. emperors
- c. the senate
- d. generals

2 In the early Roman Republic, there were:

- a. 100 senators
- b. 200 senators
- c. 500 senators
- d. 1,000 senators

3 Rome was ruled by the senate for about:

- a. 1,500 years
- b. 500 years
- c. 1,000 years
- d. 100 years

4 The richest Roman citizens were called:

- a. *plebeians*
- b. *equestrians*
- c. *paterfamilias*
- d. *patricians*

5 Number these events in Caesar's life 1–5, to put them in the correct order.

- a. He became governor of Hispania.
- b. He was elected to the senate.
- c. He visited Britain.
- d. He started the Gallic Wars.
- e. He became dictator of Rome.

6 A famous rebellion of enslaved people was led by:

- a. Crassus
- b. Pompey
- c. Spartacus
- d. Cassius

7 A famous bathhouse in Rome was built by:

- a. Constantine
- b. Caracalla
- c. Vespasian
- d. Caesar

8 Which emperor built a fortified wall in Britain?

- a. Tiberius
- b. Claudius
- c. Marcus Aurelius
- d. Hadrian

9 Which of these people were Roman emperors?

- a. Trajan
- b. Crassus
- c. Claudius
- d. Caligula
- e. Constantine

10 The last emperor of Rome was:

- a. Augustus
- b. Diocletian
- c. Romulus Augustulus
- d. Constantine

The Roman Army

Check or number the boxes to answer each question. Check your answers on page 46.

1 How many men were there in a Roman legion?

- ☐ **a.** 100
- ☐ **b.** 500
- ☐ **c.** 1,000
- ☐ **d.** 5,500

2 Which of the following was *not* a legionnaire's weapon?

- ☐ **a.** *Pilum*
- ☐ **b.** *Gladius*
- ☐ **c.** *Cingulum*
- ☐ **d.** *Pugio*

3 Who carried a century's standard?

- ☐ **a.** A centurion
- ☐ **b.** A signifer
- ☐ **c.** A tribune
- ☐ **d.** An auxiliary

4 What did each legion carry into battle?

- ☐ **a.** A golden crown
- ☐ **b.** A laurel wreath
- ☐ **c.** A silver eagle
- ☐ **d.** A *testudo*

5 A legionnaire served in the army for:

- ☐ **a.** 5–10 years
- ☐ **b.** 10–15 years
- ☐ **c.** 15–20 years
- ☐ **d.** 20–25 years

6 Which countries did most auxiliary cavalry come form?

- ☐ **a.** Gaul (France)
- ☐ **b.** Britain
- ☐ **c.** Italy
- ☐ **d.** Thrace (Bulgaria)

7 Which of the following were built by Roman legionnaires?

- ☐ **a.** Roads
- ☐ **b.** Theaters
- ☐ **c.** Bridges
- ☐ **d.** Forts
- ☐ **e.** Palaces

8 A legionnaire's durable sandals were called:

- ☐ **a.** *lorica segmentata*
- ☐ **b.** *caligae*
- ☐ **c.** *cingulum*
- ☐ **d.** *pugio*

9 Originally, how many legionnaires were there in a century?

- ☐ **a.** 50
- ☐ **b.** 100
- ☐ **c.** 150
- ☐ **d.** 200

10 Number the parts of the Roman army 1–4, from largest to smallest

- ☐ **a.** Legion
- ☐ **b.** Legionary
- ☐ **c.** Century
- ☐ **d.** Cohort

Towns and Cities

Check or number the boxes to answer each question. Check your answers on page 46.

1 Which of the following was usually found in a Roman town?

- ☐ a. A forum
- ☐ b. A *curia*
- ☐ c. A basilica
- ☐ d. A library
- ☐ e. A bathhouse

2 Semicircular Roman theaters were called:

- ☐ a. amphitheaters
- ☐ b. auditoria
- ☐ c. circuses
- ☐ d. *ludi*

3 Why were Roman road surfaces curved?

- ☐ a. So rainwater could run off.
- ☐ b. So soldiers could march on them more quickly.
- ☐ c. So they were easier to build.
- ☐ d. To help steer vehicles.

4 The most famous Roman building with a domed roof is the:

- ☐ a. Colosseum
- ☐ b. Pantheon
- ☐ c. Circus Maximus
- ☐ d. Pont du Gard

5 The city of Rome was surrounded by the:

- ☐ a. Via Appia
- ☐ b. Hadrian's Wall
- ☐ c. Aurelian Wall
- ☐ d. Via Sacra

6 A private town house was called a:

- ☐ a. *cubiculum*
- ☐ b. *domus*
- ☐ c. *atrium*
- ☐ d. *culina*

7 Which two of the following are *not* Latin names for rooms in a Roman house?

- ☐ a. *Peristylium*
- ☐ b. *Culina*
- ☐ c. *Cubiculum*
- ☐ d. *Impluvium*
- ☐ e. *Triclinium*

8 In large cities, poor people lived in apartment blocks called:

- ☐ a. *foricae*
- ☐ b. *cubicula*
- ☐ c. *tesserae*
- ☐ d. *insulae*

9 Number the stages 1–5 to show how the Romans made a mosaic floor.

- ☐ a. A pattern was drawn in the plaster.
- ☐ b. *Tesserae* were pressed into the plaster.
- ☐ c. Plaster was spread on the floor
- ☐ d. The tiles were polished.
- ☐ e. The gaps between *tesserae* were filled with plaster.

10 What was an atrium?

- ☐ a. A courtyard
- ☐ b. An entranceway
- ☐ c. A shrine
- ☐ d. A dining room

Money and Trade

Check or number the boxes to answer each question. Check your answers on page 46.

1 The first Roman coin was called the:

- ☐ **a.** aureus
- ☐ **b.** as
- ☐ **c.** sestertius
- ☐ **d.** denarius

2 The aureus was a:

- ☐ **a.** bronze coin
- ☐ **b.** silver coin
- ☐ **c.** gold coin
- ☐ **d.** lead coin

3 Which of the following might be pictured on a Roman coin?

- ☐ **a.** Gods
- ☐ **b.** Important events
- ☐ **c.** Buildings
- ☐ **d.** Emperors

4 How many asses were in one aureus?

- ☐ **a.** 100
- ☐ **b.** 200
- ☐ **c.** 300
- ☐ **d.** 400

5 What did Romans import from Syria?

- ☐ **a.** Cloth
- ☐ **b.** Glass
- ☐ **c.** Pottery
- ☐ **d.** Olive oil

6 What were Rome's two main exports?

- ☐ **a.** Exotic animals
- ☐ **b.** Wine
- ☐ **c.** Silk
- ☐ **d.** Grain
- ☐ **e.** Olive oil

7 Which of the following places supplied Rome with wool?

- ☐ **a.** Britain
- ☐ **b.** Gaul
- ☐ **c.** China
- ☐ **d.** Arabia

8 Which emperor built a huge market in Rome containing more than 150 shops?

- ☐ **a.** Augustus
- ☐ **b.** Hadrian
- ☐ **c.** Marcus Aurelius
- ☐ **d.** Trajan

9 What did the Romans use for storing olive oil?

- ☐ **a.** *Moratorium*
- ☐ **b.** *Amphora*
- ☐ **c.** *Culina*
- ☐ **d.** *Ludi*

10 How would a Roman merchant write the number 155?

- ☐ **a.** LLV
- ☐ **b.** CVV
- ☐ **c.** CLV
- ☐ **d.** CXL

Daily Life

Check or number the boxes to answer each question. Check your answers on page 46.

1 In amphitheaters and auditoria, important citizens sat:

- ☐ a. high up
- ☐ b. near the front
- ☐ c. at the back
- ☐ d. they did not attend

2 Where in Rome was chariot racing held?

- ☐ a. At the Circus Maximus
- ☐ b. At the Colosseum
- ☐ c. At the Theatre of Marcellus
- ☐ d. At the Roman Forum

3 Which of these gladiators carried a net and trident?

- ☐ a. A *secutor*
- ☐ b. A *hoplomachus*
- ☐ c. A *murmillo*
- ☐ d. A *retiarius*

4 Which two of the following weapons were *not* carried by a *secutor*?

- ☐ a. A trident
- ☐ b. A shield
- ☐ c. A spear
- ☐ d. A sword

5 When was the Colosseum completed?

- ☐ a. 80 BCE
- ☐ b. 18 BCE
- ☐ c. 80 CE
- ☐ d. 180 BCE

6 Where could Romans go to exercise?

- ☐ a. An auditorium
- ☐ b. A public bathhouse
- ☐ c. A curia
- ☐ d. A rostrum

7 What was the main meal of the day called?

- ☐ a. *Cena*
- ☐ b. *Prandium*
- ☐ c. *Palla*
- ☐ d. *Culina*

8 Who usually entertained guests at a Roman banquet?

- ☐ a. Jugglers
- ☐ b. Gladiators
- ☐ c. Dancers
- ☐ d. Clowns

9 Which of these was *not* worshiped as a god or goddess by the Romans?

- ☐ a. Neptune
- ☐ b. Mars
- ☐ c. Spartacus
- ☐ d. Venus

10 Togas with a purple band around the hem were worn by:

- ☐ a. plebeians
- ☐ b. women
- ☐ c. enslaved people
- ☐ d. senators

11 Check all the things that Roman women sometimes wore:

- ☐ a. hairpieces
- ☐ b. makeup
- ☐ c. earrings for pierced ears
- ☐ d. wedding rings

Activity Answers

Once you have completed each page of activities, check your answers below:

Pages 14–15
Finish the timeline
753 BCE City of Rome is founded.
509 BCE Rome becomes a republic, ruled by the senate.
264 BCE Rome controls all of Italy. The Punic Wars begin.
146 BCE Punic Wars end with defeat of the people of Carthage.
48 BCE Julius Caesar becomes the ruler of Rome.
27 BCE Augustus becomes the first emperor of Rome.
43 CE The Romans invade Britain.
117 CE The Roman Empire is at its height.
324 CE Emperor Constantine briefly reunites the empire.
476 BCE Romulus Augustulus loses power. End of empire in the West.

Page 15
Color the map

Page 16
Label the map of Rome
1 Theater of Marcellus
2 Pantheon
3 Roman Forum
4 Colosseum
5 Aurelian Wall
6 Baths of Caracalla

Page 17
Identify the ruin
1 Aquae Sulis baths
2 Colosseum
3 Arch of Septimius Severus
4 Pont du Gard

Page 17
When was it built?
1 Pons Aemilius (142 BCE)
2 Pont du Gard (19 BCE)
3 Colosseum (80 CE)
4 Trajan's Market (107 CE)
5 Pantheon (128 CE)
6 Arch of Septimius Severus (203 CE)

Page 18
Caesar's rise and fall
1 g
2 b
3 a
4 e
5 f
6 d
7 h
8 c

Page 19
Mix-and-match emperors
1 Augustus
2 Hadrian
3 Claudius
4 Vespasian

Page 19
The Roman Forum
1 Temple of Julius Caesar
2 Arch of Augustus
3 Arch of Septimius Severus
4 Rostrum

Page 21
Take a shopping trip
1 260 asses (18 + 24 + 4 + 48 + 6 + 160 asses)
2 140 asses

Page 22
A legionnaire's gear
1 c
2 g
3 a
4 f
5 b
6 e
7 d

Page 22
Prepared for battle
1 *gladius*
2 *pugio*
3 *lorica segmentata*
4 *cingulum*

Page 22
Packing a load
A novel and a gardening fork would not be carried in a legionnaire's pack.

Page 23
A Roman fort

Barracks (where the soldiers lived and slept)
Headquarters (central block)
Stone walls (for defense)
Gatehouse (main entrance)

Page 23
Siege warfare
a 3
b 2
c 1

Page 24
Inside a Roman town house
1 *triclinium*
2 *culina*
3 atrium
4 *cubiculum*
5 *peristylium*
6 mural
7 *impluvium*
8 mosaic floor

Page 25
How a hypocaust works
1 A fire is lit below an outer wall.
2 Heat from the fire warms the air around a series of underfloor pillars.
3 The floor heats up and causes warm air to rise into the room above.
4 Cooler air sinks and is warmed by the floor.

Page 25
Apartment living
1 *insulae*
2 five to six floors (counting the ground floor)
3 toilets
4 lower floors
5 Any two of the following:
• People used woodburning stoves to keep warm.
• There were no chimneys.
• Rooms were overcrowded, so stoves might easily get knocked over.
• The upper floors were made of wood, which burns easily.

Page 26
Pictures in stone

Roman legionnaires carrying shields and marching out of a gateway

Roman legionnaires building a fort

Roman boats tied together to form a bridge across the river

River god protecting the Romans

Page 26
Art puzzle
1 Mosaic
2 Relief
3 Cameo
4 Mural

Page 27
Mosaic mix-up
a 3
b 1
c 4
d 2

Page 28
Fashion labels
1 toga
2 stola
3 tunic
4 leather sandals
5 palla

Page 28
Sandal styles
1 c
2 a
3 d
4 b

Page 29
Fashion quiz
1 soot
2 tunics
3 Hadrian
4 purple
5 wedding rings

Page 30
Inside a Roman kitchen
a 2
b 6
c 4
d 5
e 3
f 1
g 7

Page 31
Banquet menu
Oyster, Songbirds with asparagus and quail eggs, Grapes.

Page 31
Roman food puzzle
Romans did not eat tomatoes, pasta, oranges, or bananas.

Page 32
True or false?
1 True
2 False—The letter "V" was often used instead of "U," which did not exist.
3 False—The Romans wrote on waxed tablets with a stylus.
4 True

Page 33
Number puzzle
The number 555 in Roman numerals is DLV.

Page 33
Centum puzzle
1 d
2 a
3 e
4 b
5 c

Page 34
Racing at the Circus Maximus
1 four
2 seven
3 12
4 24

Page 35
At the Colosseum
a 3
b 5
c 4
d 2
e 6
f 1

Answers

Page 35
Gladiator types
a 3
b 4
c 2
d 1

Page 36
Who's who?
1 Jupiter
2 Diana
3 Roma
4 Ancient Greeks and Etruscans
5 Mercury
6 Juno

Page 36
Praying for help
1 Venus
2 Ceres
3 Apollo
4 Neptune
5 Mars and Minerva

Page 37
Sacrifice puzzle
1 *Pontifex Maximus*
2. on altars, or in temples
3 Any two of the following: oxen, sheep, goats, pigs, chickens, doves
4. liver
5. augurs

Page 37
Making a sacrifice
a 1
b 5
c 4
d 3
e 2

Quick Quiz Answers

Once you have completed each page of quizzes, check your answers below:

Page 38
History of Ancient Rome
1 c 2 b, c 3 d 4 a 5 a 4, b 2, c 1, d 3, e 5 6 c 7 b 8 d 9 c 10 c 11 a

Page 39
Rulers and Citizens
1 c 2 a 3 b 4 d 5 a 2, b 1, c 4, d 3, e 5 6 c 7 b 8 d 9 a, c, d, e 10 c

Page 40
The Roman Army
1 d 2 c 3 b 4 c 5 d 6 a, d 7 a, c, d 8 c 9 b 10 a 1, d 2, c 3, b 4

Page 41
Towns and Cities
1 a, b, c, e 2 b 3 a 4 b 5 c 6 b 7 a, d 8 d 9 a 2, b 3, c 1, d 5, e 4 10 a

Page 42
Money and Trade
1 b 2 c 3 a, b, c, d 4 d 5 b 6 b, e 7 a 8 d 9 b 10 c

Page 43
Daily Life
1 b 2 a 3 d 4 a, c 5 c 6 b 7 a 8 a, c, d 9 c 10 d 11 a, b, c, d

---

Acknowledgments

The publisher would like to thank the following:

Alyson Silverwood for proof-reading, Philip Parker for 2020 consultant review, and Harish Aggarwal and Priyanka Sharma for the jacket.

The publisher would like to thank the following for their kind permission to reproduce their photographs:

(Key: a-above; b-below/bottom; c-centre; l-left; r-right; t-top)

Corbis: Adam Woolfitt 26tr;
DK Images: British Museum 7bc, 7cra, 21tr, 38cl; English Heritage 15cr; The Ermine Street Guard 3tr, 22c, 22ca, 22cl, 22cla, 22clb, 22cra, 22fcla, 40br, 40tc; Istanbul Archaeological Museum 16tr, 39br; Dr Simon James 34bl; Musée National du Moyen-Age, Thermes de Cluny 41b; The Museum of London 30cb; Natural History Museum, London 26br; Stephen Oliver 20cb; Rough Guides / James McConnachie 6cla, 14cla; University Museum of Newcastle 10br.

Panorama: DK Images: English Heritage / Rough Guides (Hadrian's Wall); Dr Simon James (Julius Caesar).

**All other images © Dorling Kindersley
For further information see:
www.dkimages.com**

FAMOUS STRUCTURES IN ANCIENT ROME

NAME	ARCH OF CONSTANTINE	BATHS OF CARACALLA	CIRCUS MAXIMUS
STATISTICS	DIMENSIONS 69 FT (21 M) TALL AND 84 FT (25.7 M) WIDE	BATH BUILDING 750 FT (228 M) LONG	GIGANTIC RACETRACK FOR 250,000 SPECTATORS
COMMISSIONED BY	EMPEROR CONSTANTINE I	EMPEROR CARACALLA	EXPANDED BY JULIUS CAESAR
LOCATION	ROME	ROME	ROME
DATES	COMPLETED C. 315 CE	212–216 CE	C. 50 BCE

NAME	COLOSSEUM	PANTHEON	TRAJAN'S MARKET
STATISTICS	STADIUM SEATED 50,000 SPECTATORS	DOME 141 FT (43 M) WIDE	HUGE SHOPPING COMPLEX WITH OVER 150 OUTLETS
COMMISSIONED BY	EMPEROR VESPASIAN	EMPEROR HADRIAN	EMPEROR TRAJAN
LOCATION	ROME	ROME	ROME
DATES	COMPLETED IN 80 CE	COMPLETED IN 128 CE	107–110 CE

NAME	HADRIAN'S VILLA	HADRIAN'S WALL	HOUSE OF THE FAUN
STATISTICS	ESTATE OF OVER 30 BUILDINGS COVERING 0.4 SQ MILES (1 SQ KM)	FRONTIER WALL 73 MILES (117 KM) LONG	LARGEST TOWN HOUSE IN POMPEII 32,000 SQ FT (3,000 SQ M)
COMMISSIONED BY	EMPEROR HADRIAN	EMPEROR HADRIAN	(UNKNOWN)
LOCATION	TIBUR (TIVOLI), NEAR ROME	NORTHERN ENGLAND	POMPEII
DATES	C. 120 CE	BEGUN IN 122 CE	C. 100 BCE

NAME	PONT DU GARD	TEMPLE OF JUPITER	VIA APPIA
STATISTICS	AQUEDUCT 160 FT (49 M) HIGH AND UP TO 900 FT (275 M) LONG	COLUMN HEIGHT 65 FT (20 M)	ROAD 82 MILES (132 KM) LONG
COMMISSIONED BY	MARCUS VIPSANIUS AGRIPPA (AIDE TO EMPEROR AUGUSTUS)	LUCIUS TARQUINIUS SUPERBUS	APPIUS CLAUDIUS CAECUS
LOCATION	SOUTH OF FRANCE	ROME	CENTRAL ITALY
DATES	C. 19 BCE	C. 509 BCE	FROM 312 BCE

FAMOUS ROMAN RULERS

NAME	JULIUS CAESAR	AUGUSTUS	CALIGULA
FAMOUS FOR	BEING A GREAT GENERAL	LONG, PEACEFUL RULE	BEING INSANE
TITLE	DICTATOR	FIRST EMPEROR	EMPEROR
RULED	48–44 BCE	27 BCE–14 CE	37–41 CE
LIVED	C. 100–44 BCE	63 BCE–14 CE	12–41 CE

NAME	CLAUDIUS	NERO	VESPASIAN
FAMOUS FOR	INVADING BRITAIN	BEING A TYRANT	BUILDING THE COLOSSEUM
TITLE	EMPEROR	EMPEROR	EMPEROR
RULED	41–54 CE	54–68 CE	69–79 CE
LIVED	10 BCE–54 CE	37–68 CE	9–79 CE

NAME	TRAJAN	HADRIAN	MARCUS AURELIUS
FAMOUS FOR	EXPANDING THE EMPIRE	PROTECTING THE EMPIRE WITH FORTS AND WALLS	HIS JOURNALS ABOUT PHILOSOPHY
TITLE	EMPEROR	EMPEROR	EMPEROR
RULED	98–117 CE	117–138 CE	161–180 CE
LIVED	C. 53–117 CE	76–138 CE	121–180 CE

NAME	DIOCLETIAN	CONSTANTINE	ROMULUS AUGUSTULUS
FAMOUS FOR	DIVIDING THE ROMAN EMPIRE INTO TWO: EAST AND WEST	BEING THE FIRST CHRISTIAN EMPEROR	BEING THE LAST WESTERN EMPEROR
TITLE	EMPEROR (EAST)	EMPEROR (EAST AND WEST)	EMPEROR (WEST)
RULED	284–305 CE	306–337 CE	475–476 CE
LIVED	245–313 CE	C. 274–337 CE	C. 463–476 CE